ALL YOU NEED TO KNOW ABOUT...

The Human Body

Contents

Thanks to Dr Jon Hughes

First published in Great Britain by
Cherrytree Books, part of the Evans Publishing Group
2A Portman Mansions
Chiltern Street
London W1U 6NR

Copyright © this edition Evans Brothers Limited 2004

Originally published under the title
'Mes Petites Encyclopédies Larousse Le corps'
Copyright © Larousse/VUEF 2002

Text by Agnès Vandewiele, Michèle Lancina

ISBN 1 84234 236 3

A CIP catalogue record for this book is available from the British Library

Printed in France

ALL YOU NEED TO KNOW ABOUT...

The Human Body

Illustrated by **Alice Charbin**

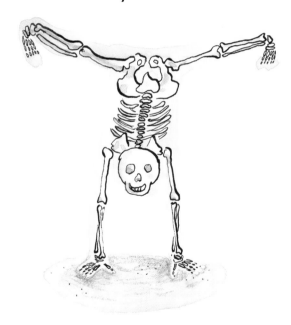

CHERRYTREE BOOKS

All different, all similar

Everyone is different: some people are tall, some are small, some are thin and some are fat. They might have fair skin or dark skin. They could have blue, brown, green or hazel eyes, curly hair or straight hair.

Even if children look like their parents or their brothers and sisters, no two people are exactly the same. Everybody is unique.

Only identical twins look exactly like each other, but their personalities can be very different.

All children are different but they are also similar: they are all made the same.

Girls and boys

Whether you are a girl or a boy, you have one head, two arms, two legs...

But a boy and a girl are not the same sex.

This means that there are some things they do in different ways – like going to the toilet!

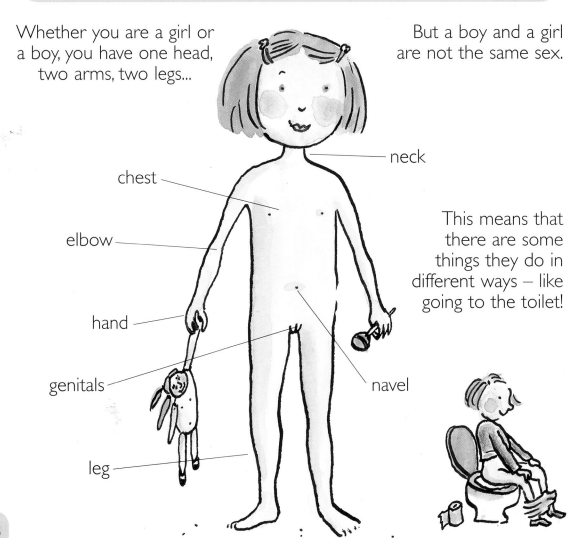

neck

chest

elbow

hand

genitals

navel

leg

Inside her body, a girl has organs that will allow her to be a mummy one day and a boy has organs that will allow him to be a daddy.

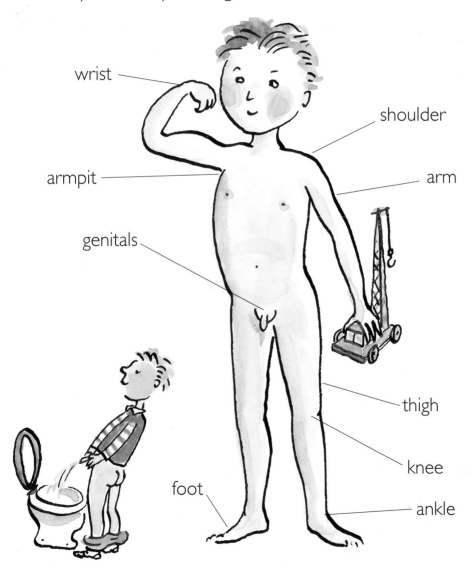

wrist

shoulder

armpit

arm

genitals

thigh

knee

foot

ankle

Skin and hair

Skin covers your whole body.
It grows with you.
It protects your body from dust, germs,
cold and heat.
Hair covers your head.

When it is hot,
you perspire.
Sweat escapes through
your pores –
tiny holes in your skin –
and cools your
body down.

When it is cold, you get goose
bumps and your pores close up.

Your skin contains a
substance that gives it
colour – this is called
melanin.
The more
melanin it contains,
the darker your
skin will be.

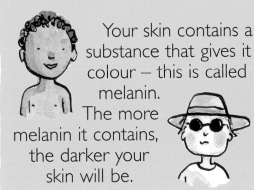

Hair grows
more
than one
centimetre
a month.

Eyebrows
and eyelashes
protect your
eyes from
dust and
water.

11

Bones and muscles

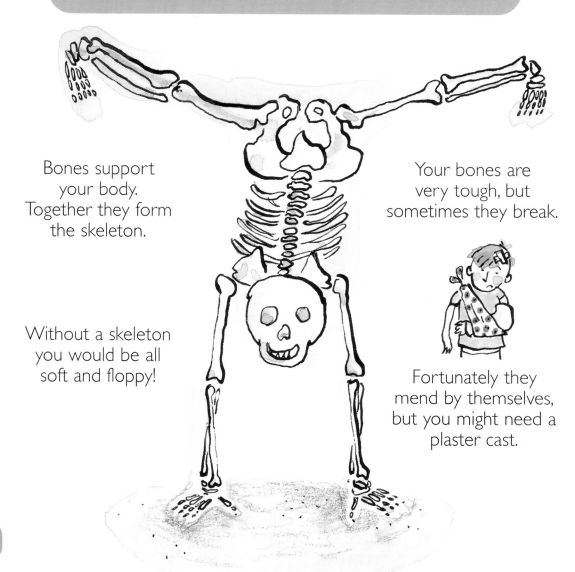

Bones support your body. Together they form the skeleton.

Your bones are very tough, but sometimes they break.

Without a skeleton you would be all soft and floppy!

Fortunately they mend by themselves, but you might need a plaster cast.

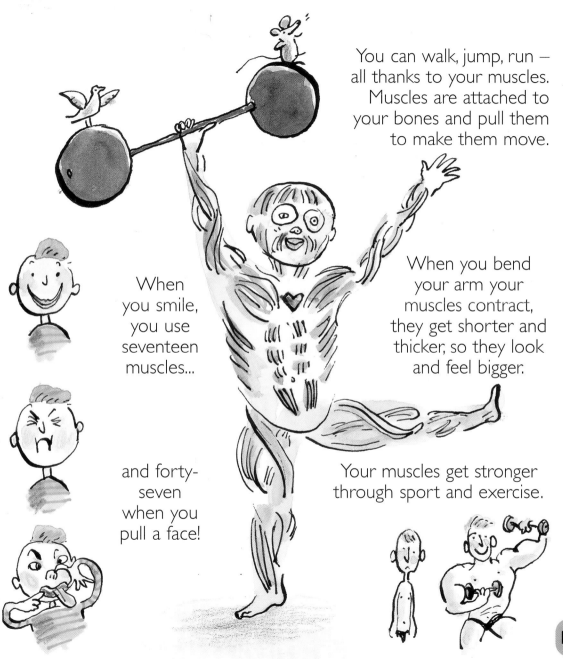

You can walk, jump, run —
all thanks to your muscles.
Muscles are attached to
your bones and pull them
to make them move.

When
you smile,
you use
seventeen
muscles...

and forty-
seven
when you
pull a face!

When you bend
your arm your
muscles contract,
they get shorter and
thicker, so they look
and feel bigger.

Your muscles get stronger
through sport and exercise.

Breathing, lungs and heart

You breathe all day and all night, and never stop. You breathe through your nose and your mouth.

Your heart never stops beating — even when you are asleep.

When you breathe, air enters your lungs and they inflate. The oxygen in the air passes from your lungs into your blood. When you breathe out, the rest of the air leaves your lungs and they deflate.

Your heart is a muscle and works all the time to send blood to the different parts of your body.

When you run you breathe more quickly and your heart beats faster, because you need more oxygen.

You can't breathe under water!

Phew, it's still there!

If you put your hand on your chest you can feel your heart beating.

Your **brain** decides everything you do

Your brain controls everything you do – thinking, moving, learning, playing, even sleeping and digesting food!

When you learn to swim or ride a bicycle, your brain remembers the movements that you have to make.

Your brain sends messages to your body very quickly if you are in danger.

When you do a jigsaw puzzle, your brain recognises the pieces that fit and instructs your hands to put them together.

To find out about the world...

...you have eyes, ears, a nose, skin and a tongue.

The black spot in the middle of your eye is called the pupil. In bright light, it gets smaller.

You see with your eyes.

Some people wear glasses to help them see better.

The circle of colour around the pupil is called the iris. This can be blue, brown, green, hazel...

Your ears hear sounds. Some sounds warn us of danger. Some people protect their ears from loud sounds.

Your tongue tells you when something is salty, sweet, bitter, hot or cold.

Your nose picks up different smells. What smells do you like best?

When you touch things, your skin tells you what is hot or cold, dry or wet, smooth or rough.

Do you like the feel of prickly skin?

Do you like the feel of being tickled?

19

Eating and digesting

You need to eat all kinds of foods to stay healthy — fruit, vegetables, meat, bread…. Foods give you protein, fat and lots of vitamins and minerals, all things that your body needs to grow properly.

Food gives your body energy.
You need to eat regularly.

You must
chew your
food properly
to help your
body digest it.

When you swallow food,
it goes to your stomach,
where it is turned into a
mush. Then it goes to your
small intestines. Here, the
parts that are good
for you enter your
bloodstream. The
parts that are not
good for you go into the
large intestine and out of
your body through the anus.

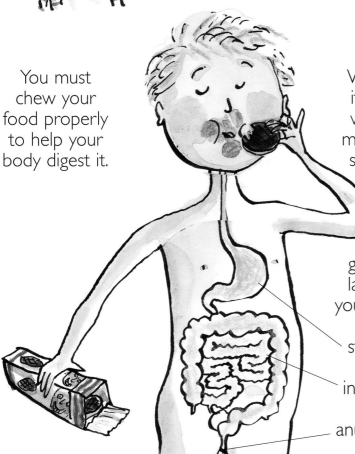

stomach

intestines

anus

21

Time for bed!

You rub your eyes, you yawn – you are sleepy. Your body needs to rest.

The younger you are, the more sleep you need, because sleep helps you to grow.

22

Your brain keeps working,
even when you are asleep.
It makes you dream.

If you dream of
something that scares
you, the dream is called
a nightmare.

Body language

Your body can show how you feel.

When you're happy, you laugh.
When you're sad, you cry.

When you're angry, you stamp your feet.

When you're in a good mood, you jump with joy.

Your face also shows how you feel.

If you're scared, you grow pale.

If you're cross, you go red.

You also make signs with your body that
help you communicate with other people.

You shake hands
to say hello.

You wave to
say goodbye.

You hug your
parents and friends
to say you love them.
And cuddles
are so nice!

When you
hurt yourself,
you cry.

Laughing can
make you
feel good.

Stay healthy!

To keep your body healthy, you should wash every day –
to get rid of dirt, sweat and germs, and to help you feel good.
Don't forget to wash behind your ears!

Remember to brush your teeth properly, otherwise they'll decay – and that hurts!

Do exercise to help develop your muscles.

When you're in the sun, protect your body: put on a hat, a T-shirt, sunglasses and sun-cream.

Do you know what's bad for your body?
Eating too many sweets.
Sitting in front of the television or computer for hours.
Not getting enough sleep.

27

Cuts and bruises

You've grazed your knee?
You should clean and disinfect
the wound to kill the germs.

If you bang your arm, a bruise
may appear. This is where small
blood vessels have burst and the
blood shows under the skin.

What a bump! Blood rushes
to where you banged your
head and you'll feel a
lump under the skin.

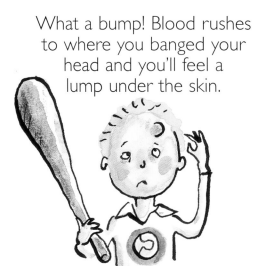

Quick! Get in
the shade!
You've got sunburn.

Insect bites can itch. A cream can help.

If your nose is running, you probably have a cold. Wipe your nose with a handkerchief!

Germs can make you sneeze. Try to sneeze into your handkerchief to avoid spreading the germs.

If a tooth decays, you might need a filling at the dentist.

Look out! Lice can jump from one person's head to another. You need a special shampoo.

If your stomach doesn't like something you have eaten, you will be sick. Sipping water can help.

If you have a nosebleed lean forward, pinch your nose and the bleeding will soon stop.

At the **doctor's**

If you feel tired and shivery you may have a fever. Your body is being attacked by germs.

To fight off the germs, your body makes lots more white blood cells very quickly, which makes your temperature rise. The doctor may give you tablets or medicine to help kill the germs and lower your temperature.

If you have a sore throat, the doctor will look in your mouth to see if you have an infection.

Some illnesses and infections can be prevented by having an injection.

Sometimes you might have to go to the hospital. Don't worry – the nurses and doctors will look after you and you'll soon feel better.

If you find yourself covered in little spots, you must see the doctor as you may have measles or chicken pox.

You get **bigger** every year

If your clothes are too small, it means you have grown.
As you grow, you learn how to do more and more things.

At about six years old,
you lose your milk teeth.

Your feet also
get bigger.

At four years
old you are twice
the size you were
at birth!

Every year you get taller and heavier.

Older girls grow breasts.

And boys grow beards.

Your body usually stops growing and changing when you are about eighteen.

33

A new baby

When a man and a woman love each other, they kiss and cuddle. They can decide to have a baby.

The daddy puts his penis inside the mummy and leaves a liquid that contains lots of little seeds, called sperm. If a sperm joins with one of the mummy's seeds, called an egg, this is the beginning of a new baby.

The baby gets everything it needs to grow through a tube called the umbilical cord. It can hear its parents' voices.

The baby grows inside the mummy's tummy, in a place called the womb, which is filled with a special liquid.

When the baby comes out of the mummy, the doctor cuts the umbilical cord, and this leaves the navel.

The day you are born is a great day! It becomes your birthday.

Records

The smallest **bone**

This is the stirrup bone, which is in the ear.

The biggest **bone**

This is the femur, the thighbone.

Eyes on the move

Your eyes move more than 100,000 times a day.

The biggest **muscle**

This is in your bottom –
your buttock muscle!

Time to **digest**

It takes a day and a night
to digest a meal.

Just **water**

More than half
of your body is
made up of water.

What a **trip!**

When we eat a mouthful of food it
travels about ten metres before it
comes out the other end!

Index